ROWING

The Experience

ROWING

ROBERT STEWART

The Experience

TEXT AND PHOTOGRAPHY BY
Robert Stewart

Published by Boathouse Row Sports, Ltd.

Dedication

To Zachary, my son. My life was blessed the day he was born.

To Frank Rich, an old and valued friend from high school. He urged me to go to the boathouse and give rowing a first try. I'm grateful that he did.

Published by Boathouse Row Sports, Ltd.
Copyright © 1988 by Robert Stewart.

Photographs individually copyrighted:
© 1988 by Robert Stewart
© 1988 by M. L. Thomas
© 1988 by Hilton Flores
© 1988 by Jon Nelson

Text copyright © 1988 by Robert Stewart.

ISBN: 0-944738-00-1

Design and production by Jon Nelson/Nelson Graphics, New Canaan, CT.
Typography by Banner Type, Westport, CT.
Printed in Japan by Dai Nippon Printing Company, Ltd., Tokyo.

Boathouse Row Sports, Ltd.
Philadelphia, PA

Contents

Foreword

Here, in photos and text as sublime a delight as the sport itself, is a striking portrayal of rowing—its camaraderie, its blinding sense of purpose, its sheer raw power and delicate movement all in one.

Robert Stewart and his contributors have used camera and language to capture the image and evoke the imagination of you, the reader. For the true glory of this sport lies in the shadows of ink on paper—in the sensing, the smells and sounds and tastes—both bitter and sweet.

Above all, below all, there is a timelessness in the medium of rowing—the waterways, the lakes and rivers—where scullers and sweep oars seek an arrangement of speed, perfect strokes, the harmony of body, soul and boat. All pass; the water holds no remembrance of things past. But you hold a primer of this passion.

Gaze at the master sculler resting on his sculls. You can feel the mature and awesome strength of legs that make his boat go with sure power. His hands, expressive and compelling...his jaw chiseled and determined...here is a champion at rest only for the moment.

And imagine the loser, the schoolboy whose head hangs forlornly. He still strains—to breathe in...shut out the vision of pain and training unrewarded when the victory went to another.

You can almost hear the ergometer wheels whirring and whining out all other surrounding sounds. Watch the blur and sense the men sweating for higher scores. And recall the silver, sparkling water of an afternoon's successful workout, yourself feeling the external pleasures this sport offers.

Internally, you experience rowing as a graphic microcosm of life— solitude, learning, work, rest, nourishment, sharing—and ultimately challenge.

Not everyone wins, and certainly not everyone wins all the time. But once you get into your boat and push off, tie into your shoes and bootstretchers, then "lean on the oars," you have indeed won far more than those who have never tried.

ALLEN P. ROSENBERG
Coach, Vesper Boat Club's Olympic
Gold Medal Men's Eight-Oared Shell
XVIII Olympiad, Tokyo 1964

The Making of an Oarsman

M. L. THOMAS

An oarsman trains to row like a symphony musician: committed, focused, often possessed by purpose. Both know artistry and hard work. But the oarsman may have the edge; he also invests sweat—psychological and physical.

The places where oarsmen train are distant from rowing's pageantry and cheering crowds. Virtually every oarsman has known the "tanks," where many intercollegiate rowers spend much of their indoor training. Barbells slam hard on the wooden floor as crews—men and women—pump weights until it's their turn to row. Cadences and instructions from coaches punctuate the whine of the

water-circulating machine. Bodies grunt and faces grimace.

Outdoors, rowers run up hills and stadium steps. Again. And again. A trip to the top of some of those steps is proof that the mason poured them as much with punishment as with concrete.

Training also means the ergometer, a machine that promises pain without Olympic medals yet spits out data that predict Olympic performance.

Most of all, oarsmen row countless miles. Seat races that separate the good from the best. Boats spread across a river, with crews working on their starts. And coaches sitting in their launches—watching, instructing, and sometimes cajoling.

When technique becomes flawless and physical endurance long-lasting, the sculler is virtuoso; the crew, an orchestra performing to ''bravo!''

''Rowing is more than a fast boat on race day. It's a complementary experience to a young man's intellectual development.

''Rowing, like success, is a journey, not a destination. I tell my oarsmen to have fun, learn and, most of all, grow as individuals. The wins and losses will take care of themselves.''

RICK CLOTHIER
Rowing Coach,
United States Naval Academy

ROBERT STEWART

ROBERT STEWART

Oarsman

"I still recall Ernie Arlett's words to us one day during practice as undergraduates at Northeastern. 'Gentlemen, on the way back, I want you to row as if you are fairies dancing on the water.'

"It gave me the lasting impression that we were, in fact, trying to slide this boat along the water more as a ballet than a slugfest. And he was our masterful choreographer."

LARRY GLUCKMAN
Varsity Heavyweight Coach
Princeton University

ROBERT STEWART

ROBERT STEWART

''Rowing is not like baseball, where you can arrive late, grab your glove and run onto the field. For me, it was the discipline of having to be at a given place at a given time, sometimes seven days a week.

''As time went on, that very discipline influenced other dimensions of my life.''

FRANK SHIELDS
Pennsylvania '63

"As a coxswain, I concentrated most on knowing the people in my boat—why they were rowing, why they came down to the boathouse, what made them tick.

"You have to know whether someone's rowing becauce they love their mother and hate their father. They're not sure they are proud of themselves; they want to be proud.

"Determine some of that and you can tap the strongest parts of those individuals. Being able to inspire someone, unexpected and in a way new and fresh to them, is what made coxswaining special for me."

DEVIN MAHONY
Coxswain, Varsity
Heavyweight Eight
Harvard '86

ROBERT STEWART

M. L. THOMAS

Tools

HILTON FLORES

ROBERT STEWART

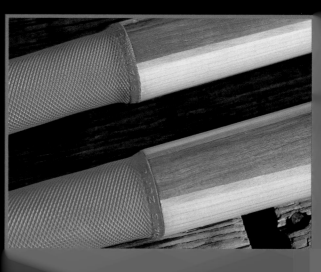

M. L. THOMAS

III

The Boathouse & Tradition

ROBERT STEWART

Walk into a boathouse sometime when no one is around. The locker rooms and boat bays seem to almost speak in dignified tones. The sport of rowing is the language; pride and tradition, its dialect.

Whether a century old and graced with finely detailed woodwork or new—made of brick and steel, the boathouse is more than a storehouse for boats and oars between regattas. It is an entryway to the lineage of rowing, its doors opening to anyone who wants to row and grow into that proud lineage.

With passing years, boathouses themselves grow into comfortable dwellings where generations of crews and scullers come to learn and

compete. The hardwood floors lose
their varnished reflection. Here and
there, paint begins to peel from
beams and joists. Yet the lustre
remains in a highly polished plaque
dedicated to a coach or boatwright
who once inspired rowers. Perhaps a
paper poster or silken banner recalls
a great regatta from the past.

Old and new intermingle. Odors of
yesterday's gasoline, epoxy and river-
sodden rags waft through the boat
bays, while coxswain megaphones of
yesteryear hang in the repair room.
Old oars and shells recall the days
when wood was the only material to
test a rower's skill. Black and
yellowing white photographs of
yesterday's champions line the walls
in dusty frames. Not old and
forgotten faces; only well-worn by
time and distinction. And racing
shells bear the names of individuals
and teams that enriched rowing's
heritage.

These are the collective hallmarks
of tradition, the most enduring
threads of rowing's fabric.

Athletes remember the people,
events and surroundings that came
together so a crew could row to
victory. And the boathouse, with
racing shells in their berths and the
bulletin board by the pay phone on
the wall, is where today's sweat,
determination and cheers join
yesterday's legends.

Tradition

41

ROBERT STEWART

ROBERT STEWART

Tradition

43

ROBERT STEWART

ROBERT STEWART

ROBERT STEWART

Rowing

52

Tradition

SPIRIT OF '55

Rowing

IV

Regatta

M. L. THOMAS

ROBERT STEWART

M. L. THOMAS

Rowing

ROBERT STEWART

ROBERT STEWART

ROBERT STEWART

''On race day, there's tremendous anxiety. Leading up to the stake boat, I distinctly remember saying to myself, 'I can't wait till this is over.' ''

FRANK SHIELDS
Pennsylvania '63

They sit motionless, momentarily frozen in their seats. Knees are flexed, arms extended, fingers wrapped around thick oar handles.

This is the starting line at a rowing race.

Holding the starter's flag above his head in one hand and a megaphone to his mouth in the other hand, the race official will call scullers and crews to their contests: "Sit ready. . . ready all. . .row!"

The rowers explode in recoil—back, then forward, like synchronous pistons in a high-performance engine.

A rowing race is a series of almost simultaneous contradictions. An oarsman's individuality coexists with the wholeness, the unity of everyone together in the boat rowing as one precise machine.

A crew's rhythm may be smooth for a series of strokes yet suddenly come apart. One oar blade drops into the water too late or too soon, of seven others together and without imperfection. The rhythm is broken, the momentum gone. Races are sometimes won and lost by such narrow margins of error.

Despite the physical toll—fatigue, pain, muscles struggling against oxygen debt—the shift into kinetic movement seems almost effortless.

When it works, rowing as a process manages to transform from the roughness of two powerful animals fighting one moment to the smooth gracefulness of a ballerina's aerial leap the very next.

Some see the paradox of a rowing race as an almost metaphysical test. Row with great skill, they say, and you will know the sensation of "rowing within yourself"—at one with the boat, the crew, the oar and the water.

HILTON FLORES

M. L. THOMAS

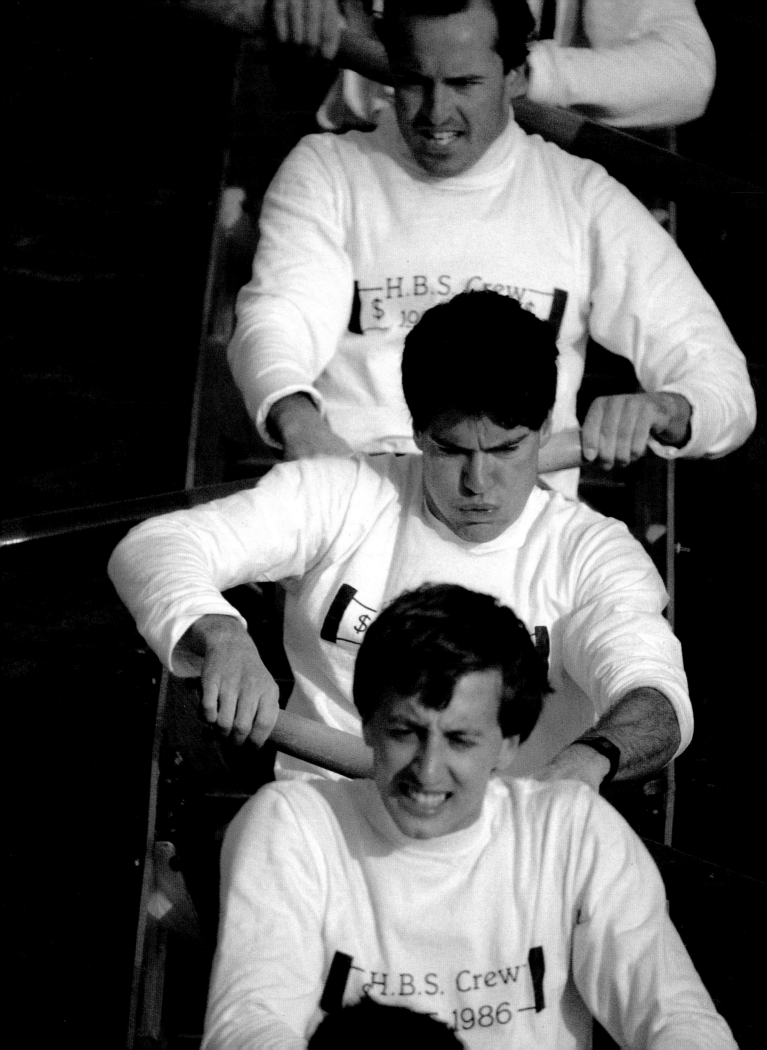

HILTON FLORES

JON NELSON

"In rowing as in life, there are competitors and there are racers. The competitor works hard and rows to his limit. The racer does not think of limits, only the race."

JIM DIETZ
Rowing Coach
United States Coast
Guard Academy

ROBERT STEWART

"The most significant message I can convey to the rowing athlete is: Just row the race. Think about the process. Don't dwell on the result until it's history."

LARRY GLUCKMAN
Varsity Heavyweight Coach
Princeton University

Regatta

93

ROBERT STEWART

ROBERT STEWART

ROBERT STEWART

ROBERT STEWART

ROBERT STEWART

Rowing

102

M. L. THOMAS

Rowing's Faces

ROBERT STEWART

Rowing

ROBERT STEWART

ROBERT STEWART

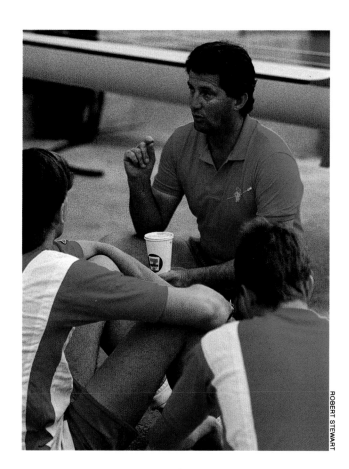

ROBERT STEWART

ROBERT STEWART

ROBERT STEWART

HILTON FLORES

ROBERT STEWART

VI

Single Sculls

ROBERT STEWART

It is daybreak on a winter morning in the cities of Philadelphia, Washington and Boston. The temperature outside is close to freezing, and the barometer is falling, hinting possibly at snow. Most people are inside—rising from sleep, brewing some coffee—and beginning the day in warmth.

Then, there are the others. They walk out of boathouses into the morning's rawness and place wood or fiberglass single sculling shells into the cold waters of the Schuylkill, Potomac and Charles rivers. They slip their oars, or sculls, through riggers and fasten the oarlocks.

The time has come to focus on one thing; rowing. The power from strong

and well-trained arms, legs and backs renders the unpleasant weather into simply a nuisance, never a hardship.

A sculler's world of solitude, serenity, mental concentration and contest with the river's waters is too intense, too self-absorbing to allow any distractions from nature's elements.

Everything besides rowing is, at these moments, inconsequential. There is only the water, the boat, the individual and the experience.

Why do they row, especially by themselves? For some, it is exercise, readying for competition, recreation, even perhaps therapy because they are handicapped. For others, it is personal time and personal space.

Whatever the reason, a sculler rows like an artist paints; it never ceases being a special individual experience.

ROBERT STEWART

"It's impossible to describe the enormous feeling of rowing through a patch of leaves floating on the water while darkness is seconds away. You just shoot through them, and the sensation feels much faster than your actual speed."

STUYVESANT PELL
University Barge Club
Princeton University Rowing Association

Single Sculls

HILTON FLORES

ROBERT STEWART

Rowing

126

"Rowing is a sport for dreamers. As long as you put in the work, you can own the dream. When the work stops, the dream disappears."

JIM DIETZ
Rowing Coach
United States
Coast Guard Academy

Single Sculls

Acknowledgments

M. L. THOMAS

I especially wish to thank John Bannan,
Bill Leavitt, Stan Bergman, Larry
Gluckman, Charlie Butt and Curtis
Jordan for their considerable
cooperation as I produced this book.

They are among many other people in
the rowing community I have met since
early 1985 who each generously helped
me with this project.

ROBERT STEWART
July 1987